MW00979117

For Lack of a Canary

Mark DeCarteret

Nixes Mate Books
Allston, Massachusetts

Book design by d'Entremont
Cover photograph courtesy of State Library and Archives of Florida.

Thanks to Sam Cornish for getting me started and setting me on the right course, Deke and Sandra, my parents, for all types of support, The City Hall Poets, for their top notch suggestions and guest-starring, Jim Rioux, for his championing of my work and my person, and Kathleen, for her unmatchable skills as an editor and her unstoppable grace, love.

ISBN 978-1-949279-00-9

Nixes Mate Books
POBox 1179
Allston, MA 02134
nixesmate.pub/books

In memory of Bill Knott

Contents

For Lack of a Calling

For Lack of a Calling

Neither the bird's birth –
its tiny heart like a device's light,
this warning of sorts

or its chirping –
the tongue like a worm now
that is trying to lure out another bird's signal

and not so much its soul
but more the delight of its singing –
all its note-starts and stops, its distant harmonies

whether perched in the thistle
like a chorus line or in flight –
we are listening in with our not-so-songs

though somehow the sun's still sounded out –
the sum of that waning light
we have heard the world speaking about

for the birches would seem to know
more about the weather than the snow
and the clouds put together

either that or my silence
has won over the universe and it's I
that am lending it my view of the sky.

The Farewell Season

I've been paired up with the earth much too often,
my body, year after year, chummier with its peat-stink –
here, where the ferns are nefariously threaded tight
and the newts safe guard its most comical songs –
but back, mattering less, festering, spring after
spring, as if I'm the smuggler's redolent stash,
being smacked against the butt end of history.
Rocks play dumb. And trees have stopped keeping score,
having been twisted into crosses out next to the parking lot
where the car-tops are worried with crow-crap.
South, there's a thousand more like me. And north,
they can't tell us from the voices the wind's thrown.
Only the river's been insistent, turning out more of itself,
ceaseless and vacant-eyed, only detouring for love,
to catch up on more of the sea and its past lives.
I cock my head, gumming some remedy, growing
simpler by the minute but only when I'm half-in-it.
My mug shots droop down like moss. I've the skin-tint
            of porridge.
And have spent the last hour giving lap dances to
            tree-stumps.
O, you who've fared better, breathe deep for me –
those few who raft air, who are wafted, whisked-off,

be sure to roach-clip my remains and sample some of
          my plaint
when I've bottomed out, un-noteworthy and furred,
finally nailing my poet-role and rough-drafting towards
          lore.

Guides

When we're not weighing in
on our own lives, the world,
we will take notes on nature –
try tagging or getting at it
with arrows, gold embossment,
the somber netting of logbooks,

like those two godwits we ogled
then shored up with our dashes,
rush ordered into these holdings –
the uninhabitable white, the what-of-it,
as they waded in a lacquer-shine,
what's recalled of dawn's yellows

till their bodies, so apt at stillness,
were wet twine, our entryway's tile,
their bills, sky-turned, stirring
up that same tide-diet, flesh –
little now but a sighting, its afterglow,
words filtered from light, giving way.

The Fall II

Out back is crammed with dead leaves –
clues to their last bout with a troubling cold,
and a sound not unlike Auden clearing his throat.
Where I walked earlier there are claw-marks
and the indentations left from my staff.
O Lord, I've grown fat on the wrong words
and come noon, I'll have been sent more articles
letting me know how the talks have stalled,
that the crates of water will arrive late again,
as well as the doves, who'll look cooler-headed
than I do, when saved to the side of a vase.
Only light has tried to straighten itself out –
taking even less time with the lake's surface, tile.
We ask so little of creation. Outside all of it.

A Good Day

to Jim Harrison

To live, I've been left blank
giving up on the idea of evil, mediocrity.
So, so much for the shoreline
or the hutch I've inherited from my parents
where I keep things I've collected there.
A blue die with its eye blackened out.
A piece of paper doubling as a swan.
A pink golf ball labeled "Can't Miss."
Why is it my poems have cheapened with time,
lapsed like snow, are desire-less, while yours
have been raised up, said, with so many last breaths?
My sky is picked over. No stars
to rate what I've artfully clamored for,
no gods in the market for my emptied cart.
I'm growing sore from all this asking.
When the world doesn't want what you have
you eat fast food, attract viruses.
But in your final clip, you are scratching
your ass against a plum blossom.
Bumming a cigarette off of the world.
And leaving nothing in the way of wine.
Free of shake-ups and cleanses and passwords

you resist the camera's reassurances, ever-readiness,
and burn as only the fitfully sacred can.
Issa's horse doesn't know a brick
from a bible, a car alarm from a liberal,
doesn't read into the rain, weep itself crib-sick or blind.
I'm waking startled like an immigrant uncle.
Incisions made in my head. My dreams missing.
But sharing this lack with the angels now.

The Great Disappointment

Just a few weeks ago I was walking off winter
like the twin crows I saw in their coal miner black
out next to some snow, a Tums-white, muttering,
another readout of hexes and pin numbers,
demands from the ex-wives of prognosticators,
as if emboldened by a string of low 60's –
the sun suddenly cued amidst near-rabid suds,
and the trees upset and tipped at the shins,
this one pine so much so there's that nip-bottle scent,
until at a loss, I sat dolman-style, smelling like
lichen, almost soulful when taken in at a slant.
Did in by my tan lines I'd been ID'd but was still a put-on
even having signed the prenups with my suffering self.
Anything I'm not lacking has been historically uncalled for.
For who, descended from star-stuff, then fussed-over,
and eventually tar-pitted, brains blessedly at rest,
can bear up beneath any god crabbed above us,
weigh-in (one's writing hand cramped into fist) –
on even some wet bark or deer crap, the erstwhile light,
those newts of one's youth, too shy or too few, never
mind about swallowing one more mark-up of hell?
But still there will be film at eleven. Atoms
riffing off of each other. Some even resembling heaven.

And I'll thrive like the ants on my son-in-law's roses
        again...
sorry my mistake, they appear to be merely coffee grounds
either shuffled by wind or the sneeze of the knelt-down.
He has been crucified a dozen so times more than Christ
if you count the amateur competitions, sundry dry-runs.
Once upon a time I stood up for a few truths,
regardless how populated by talking trees, dated –
indicted in ink at least the color of thought
or chiseled into one ton stone where the rain
would eventually side with it, S down, then swell.
For what do fools know about ice ages, poisonous gas?
We all thumb through the passages on smarts the same
        way,
much rather falling for the laugh of the overseer,
        law-giver,
than listening for the slipper-steps, sighs, from one-of-
        our-own.

The Idea of Order in Florida

After tipping the dead pit bull
into a canal already filled with them
I attempt to rub out the garish blooms
that my mother's weekly rags,
with snapshots of stars slapped and palsied,
had left behind on my forearms.
Flies too are making track marks
on what once had been billed as water,
and an iguana is thawing itself
on a half-submerged shopping cart –
the poor thing with no fight left,
each of its claws filed down
to the most trifling lines in a Stevens' ode.
Listen and the wind will dish out
on all Wallace's tried-n-true tricks, his fad dieting,
will sing of the sea ever-burning, out-of-key.
Shouldn't rage be less dignified, cruder?
I am done rhyming with what-not,
hiring on his most unnecessary of gods.
There is more crap in his attic –
crates of mentholated rub and remotes,
an acre of settees, old test scores –
than a theme park or ocean floor.

I dance around a red stain of ants,
then read up on this cypress –
how its under new management,
its future appearing to be even eerier
with this strangler fig flattering it.
Clouds tail off in a tractor tread.
The sun lists its maladies, silently.
I duck under the on-ramp construction
its hundred-sung greeting of rubber,
its temple-like coolness and letting-up,
and look past where these shadows pool,
the future forever unschooled in the past,
to where these two ospreys stay posted,
the scales of the fish in one of its grips
no less resplendent than estate jewels.

In Defense of Thomas Bernhard's Soul

1453 could've been the day before yesterday
and let's say oblivion the day before that.
With that in mind, the wind sure feels pleasant.

I hold off swallowing the olive because
it strikes me as the right thing to do,
almost Christ-like in some light.

What risk is there filing one's life under sleep?
Or to sleep like the pulse-less, kissed-off?
For the sleeper is at home in heaven as in hell.

Lead me to those most pliable of memories
or if you wish just the moon – the shined-up
side one can only see when standing here.

The best of lines come like a door-stopper.
When lashed to no one god's mast the seas
are not so much open as unfazed, bluest-blue.

I was lent ten times this in happiness.
I fattened-up, grew ever-mightier, on happiness.
Nothing looks dafter on the page than happiness.

Ever since I put out the new mat I've been
kept up all night by its ceaseless pleading.
May it be washed of my sins and the sins of my friends.

Please, tell me I haven't lost you. Are we not
so much made, wrestling free from damnation,
as forever dreamt-up, taking one for the team?

A creak in the board swears it would not let me fall.
All well and good but will I have the words for it?
No, the best lines come like the prettiest of swords.

Key West, January 7, 2010

One rooster sneezes non-stop
and another dribbles blood
down the front of its chest.
Tell me what use is a bird at this hour
unless it be clearing its throat of our woes?
The noise from the bar kept us up again.
That Billy Collins impersonator blow-
drying those poems he'd left out
on the deck overnight and a pirate
testing his sword on the sole of his Ked.
The entire state's under a cold snap,
the local news uncrating its arctic-
white captions, oft-panning
to the crops doubling over –
miles of oranges enduring the ice,
their skin this refrigerator-finish.
So how much of this tropical print
haven't we dreamt-up before –
only more lurid, a direr red?
Insects grow more listless on the sills
and breezes chill our smiles into zeros.
I have been utterly underutilized here.
Cocked to the sky, a vowel's open throat –
not so much a becoming, this cosmic comb-over
as something asterisked taking on absence.

The Last Day of Christmas

Earlier, I'd ladled dead mayonnaise
into the sink – eggs ever the informants,
so as to recycle the plastic container,
and then did time with yet another poet
wanting to be my estranged mother.
Eighteen miles from the sea (when in
reality have we ever referred to it as *the sea?*)
and still the gulls huddle, reading for their parts on the
          roof,
too cold to even bully any room at the feeder.
More neighbors will be lugging bags of wrap to the
          cul-de-sac.
One clad only in thermal underwear, patched jacket,
talking about duct taping the mouth of a loud dog.
Another handing me a flyer lousy with used gum.
Maybe I should introduce my soul on a dare.
And afterwards make raids on some variety store
          dumpster,
a 70's security camera trained on my activities,
this sound like big fish gills clicking open and closed.
Instead sparrows will rouse in the eaves, dallying
longer than usual, in their outdated wear.

The sky so dull our kisses seem rave-induced.
And there will be that sour inquisition of sleep again,
my eye-lids dialing up some prototype of peace.
Why am I late getting to most everything?
Putting away the cot, slept-in linens.
Stocking up on more top round and catsup.
Maybe I'm saving myself for the poet's last task,
all that volunteering I've been thinking of doing.
Or for taking in the lights. Once the sun
has had at them a little while longer.

Men as Enemy of Birds

Over the speaker we hear the wood stork –
its legs, swizzle-stuck, eyes, burnt-cork black,
neck, this high school machine-shop mishap,

as it chokes on a billion years of sugar crops, chaw
with nary a bucket of water to be straw-sucked.
What wasn't thawed on Formica for me or

morphed into a hat for you, has been turned inside-
out and mounted, posed as if nothing is happening.
Here, buttons do everything but ad lib, see us

out towards the deck's stenciled dribble and scat,
where, no doubt, all these sawdust-fed bodies
will be sung a ways into the field, resurrected.

The sky is first gun barrel then flask-glint –
later, snake-scales and lastly, can-top or tinsel.
And I regret now not stopping at the Tram Mart,

not arming myself with more minutes and breath mints.
You observe the same regret but are logging it

"SHAME –
a mesh-like sensation of loss that doubles as soul."

A pick-up truck backs up to an airbrushed shrub,
dropping off tubs of artillery and sport drinks.
And another eco-safari van is idling in the lot.

Trees not from these parts are strapped in,
plastic tabs where there leaves had been.
Some mosses, the color of meat cooked well done,

hang like streamers. Others, iron, like chains.
I'm asked to play the role of a trapper, you, a parrot.
Things we didn't think interactive now have it in for us,

making it difficult to tuck back our hair, take in air.
A heron, stucco-white, tidies up its display case.
It gets by on "a diet of tide-sounds and saddest of scripts –

the most silent of vowels like an italicized essing-
out through the algae – its wings forever at-a-loss."
I try to put my finger on its timeline, you, its disfiguring.

Me?

I conjure a just-risen sun
and the purest of snows
stirred up by two juncos.

And the world?

Only this white screen
and/or the words it lures out:
a nuclear plant's test siren.

Nature Show as a Sacred Act

Light dwindling like it does when the wind
smells of elm-leaf slowly drawing toward yellow,
the old man imagines lobbing a bottle –
the tint of some fabled sky, far-off sea –
into the space where a loon calls
off-beat with its breath, before he tries
to bow to the fits of spray, cold,
the oft-rapping, stiffening sails, of the boats
as if it the start of something near sacred
like those hosts with their whispered narrations
who've been pressing for sainthood since the 70's.

But let's stop before we get carried away –
the lips forming around sentiment or even
dining on the salt that outlasted most of what's
passed for a meaningful phrase or a kiss,
and get back onto the step where he's petting
a lost cat or stalled over a third glass of wine
or better yet, turn our sights to where the alewife
keep filing up ladders, all knife-glint and factual,
and some osprey, dumbstruck by its luck,
takes one more commercial up on its offer,
poses, for yet another of its followers.

Nine Lives into It

I'll mostly lie to the cat. About
the illness. Where the pills are at.

Lies that leave spots.
Lies that opt into spittle.

I'll let it have the whole bed.
And pat it while it sits on the sill.

There's either this silence. Or that channel where
they're always selling you something for less.

And always its eyes like these lemon-lime coasters.
Its lips like spilt ink. Its tiny teeth, Tic Tacs.

I'll lie down, still thinking, until I hear tapping.
Those pink pads of ghosts. Acting up yet again.

"The One Absent from All"

No, not the same butterfly as the last poem –
that blue I'd referred to as "a heaven twice-sacked,"

this silver I'd dubbed "a butler-shined knife,"
or the feverish prying at a bud I had bluffed –

the asthmatic heaves and uneasiness I flubbed
measuring up against my own un-surety, strife

or worse, used as a case study for my sanity's sake,
this relic I'd sworn to and cared for in line after line,

would continue to see to its damnable flowers,
so mad about their beauty, so adamant it was mine.

Off Seasonal Affective Disorder

You tiger-ripped through spring again
still anger-tinged, griping, about winter

and its negating winds, sinless-ness, though
toughening up on all things winged and raw

trying to put a new spin on the robins at war,
the seed boring up through the endless epics

and the bloodroot that tenses-up and broods,
indestructible as Tupperware, at your door,

before robbing the earth of its nutrients, turnings,
being somewhat inspired by Rimbaud's mad spider,

the web it's tie-dyed in these assorted blacks,
and assuming the glare of some smuggler-muse,

the unwell and oft-yellowing input of summer.
One can either fall laughed-at or rot torch-sung.

Page for What Little Has Been Grasped

We read up on the two or three histories
that hadn't been burnt or swept out to sea.

Here, the roads always turn towards the sun
so one has the clearest view of the rubble.

Once a deer surfaced from out the waves of light
and then bowed down, so close we could hear it.

Later, we curled up on the remains of a pew
in what was once a church, was once sleep.

Rye Harbor, August 27, 2005

Trapped in a tidal pool, late August,
at that starless letting-up of twilight,
a tuna tested the yet unseen moon
as if sensing its pull and its whitish start,
turning towards future perfect, its fin
this titanium accessory, tensing up
as it lapped again, silently powered,
having already refused the sun and its past-
takes —its latest run of sufferings and rust,
and making even less of the water's indifference –
its tone flattening, note by note, over time,
or the setting, those like-minded stones
with their cold stare and depth,
that unsettling algae atop most of them,
the fish opting to step it up, circling "yes" in ink
as imperceptible as these spectators' thinking
so there was nothing left for our cameras to see
but our own flashes, half-imagined tempests.

Rye Harbor, September 1, 2005

Finally, I'm of the mind to submit
to that shore – the earth itself finished,
indeterminate in the deafening surf, mist.
Even with the late afternoon sun
and the hundreds of dragonflies
it has flagged in the tall grass and phlox
I've had my fill of the eternal debate.
Let all the tabbed and the filed-away
tell it one final time before becoming
stalled in mock-reflection, battered clean.
Ten or so gulls flank the only outlet.
One lifts up into the air with a cell phone,
another, a bag leaking something black.
I'm up to my ankles in plankton and fleas,
the canned talk of lost men and their boats.
Who wouldn't crumble, come to blows, in such murk?
The terns laugh and I fall in line, staring
sternly at the Styrofoam floats and torn nets.
I'm so out of touch with my own story
my hands are now literally rotting.
A shout comes from down on the rocks.
This small fox soft-pads up through where
the sand is mostly texts about the weather, foam,
except for where the mad have had at it.

Return

to where the walnuts have been gutted
and your law books teeth-tugged towards the evergreens
to be wrung into wreaths, versed in bloodier intonations,
to where you'd seen ten or so turkeys burst forth
from the scrub, lurch across the white crust
and curse your gods beneath their breath,
or return to where cardinals, bled-targets,
have regained the sewer grate, borrowing
from the sun and its unwavering brow-beating,
or the snow's gone an overdubbed gray where it's rutted
and given to shadow, the dashes lent wordlessness,
but return, nonetheless – with the grunts, urgent strides
of a boy growing sorrier, ever-worried with his worsening
      diet,
to where nature is not always blown-up, then doctored,
then blown-up again.

Solstice

to Pat Parnell

The world has left off at the forest's lip,
slipping past where there is any known season
at the plastic fence power-sprayed its original white,
the flag wavering between arisen and winded.

I can still see a passing figure, a little of the street,
where these teens have graffitied our sign again,
and come December, once the trees are bare,
where the deer will steal apples as soft as bagged sap

and maybe the grass, this brown worn by mystics,
being urged towards the winter by grubs again,
or even some violets contemplating their names,
the flawed reason of their half-toppled pots.

And though where I stand barely any light's met,
I can scare up enough to read up on the sun's path
so what hasn't yet scattered, raced off for the dark,
can be given over to the care of those still inclined.

The Sea Watchers

Between white caps tamed into form
and tidal grasses plugged into place
we'll opt for spaces unmated to gesture.
No we haven't been us, never mind, you or me.
This, the kind of light, rid of weekend frivolity,
fired up from that original ring in this direst grip,
the kind of light even Hopper wouldn't pose us.
Something worms up from out tomorrow to hand-signal us.
Is it those words I lack breath for or haven't once risked
or the eulogized blue of a Provincetown sky?
A bittern tries to blend in with what's left of dusk,
forgoing, just this once, its diet of retro-browns, rust.
I try to trace its beak with a stiffened wrist,
and with that failing, lift the first one I see on the internet.
Another mansion stammers out towards the bluff
as if it can see in its own picture windows
the same masterworks, ego, as Nature.
What in God's name ever drew us here?
How this backdrop can't be bothered to preen, go in
for re-fittings, instead always, training on silences, fasting?
A kingfisher is shivering on the edge of a shed,
so in-time and key it looks Auto Tuned to our desires.
You ask if in this vastness some permanence might be
starved out. Never, I say. As if I knew
the first thing about preservation.

At Stratham Hill Park

Even in the steadiest of rains
on my sixth or seventh jumping jack
my legs were electric with ticks again,
their bodies doubling over with blood
all a-tremble like gelatin on my skin.
Now, the trees are swaying just the way
that you said they would and the air's
thick as sap in that designated pasture,
the sun surrounded with no-see-ums,
a couple of clouds appearing out-of-sorts, sulking.

You say "stay" and it's as if I am suddenly tased,
none of that teeth-clicking, picnic-table-tapping
I'd been written up for so much in the past
as I sat in the pavilion and listened to blue jays
at war and then noted how the sparrows were not
(jotting down how they dipped for a piece of chip
before returning to the rafter's all clotted with web
one brown as drab and uninspiring as the other –
in the beautifully crafted, heartfelt words of some bard).
Yes, love, I'll be leaving. I'll be all that is left.

Tahoma

The same ad for dawn again. How I've mastered
its theme song but not the game show that follows.
One day I will wake without any knack for words,
ransoming canned ones in some random order.
Sad, how the littler the heart the less easy it's tamed,
how the mind will go dim when we need it the most.
So I'll lip-synch another April still unripe on the page,
sounding its peeled skin into pyres to be lit.
Anything not solid is at a loss, given to the smoke
that rises in off-white drifts, those poor comatose souls.
If you must purge please purge as a group I tell myself.
For only our fingernails are left to grin and/or tap out
irony for those who pick up on these type of things.
Yes, light has fallen. Targeting the power lines, pine trees.
What isn't gray will be torn up into rags.
Even the shell-glint and leg-splints of pigeons,
the clouds secretly recorded for their off-color asides.
We standardized snow for this reason alone –
tired of it lounging around in its underwear, ever-sighing.
Sorry for the interruption. We'll now return you to your
        poem.
Listen though and you might hear where I've been
        fooling
around with my first metaphor, grafting tedium to sun,
trading this most earnest of fonts for something aloof.

The Temptation of St. Anthony
at Hampton Beach State Park

A late sun pans the ruler-straight shoreline –
this spire thrusting up like a strap-on,
these four shacks snapped half-assed into place,
but then stops, opting to cash in
on a lure snug in a statue's lap,
then showcases a gull as it struts around
after rapturously tapping into a soft drink.
I sidestep your pet – its ankles sudsy, rump a-steam,
half-stumbling like some fresh penitent
dumped on the street in a temple-fog
sharing his goofy smile, rash, with the sinners
and then trying to rest in this shadiest of spots
where gum wrappers are pasted
like late petals to the white path,
and rosehips, aroused by their own thorns,
part again from their sorest-red ripening.
I look away, not entirely stable, to a law-beset wall,
cooling to those mock gods and their come-ons,
as these bats, saturated with dusk, take
stabs at another of my so-called haloes.

Test Poem

Another star is ushered off the fake velvet display.
That would make eleven. Or twelve if we toss in the
        plane
that's long sought to eavesdrop on the heavens.

Most of what half-fazes us happens well over our heads.
Oh, what a push it all is. What a lowering of trust.
I plead that you remove everything in the log up till now,

when I'll try to gaze out with more gravity, leverage.
No, no, no – shushing the dog doesn't do any good.
On the way down the stairs I will still rough up its fur

and point out those gums as black as turned fruit,
how it struts towards the entryway turf then attacks it.
Even my touch is a kind of evasion, cutback in feeling.

I've been left to that self I have fled since the casino
        arrest.
All trace of the others deleted from my cart.
The sky is toy-gun gray. Ask again, rag-burnished.

And the clouds have that same disarmingly rigged look
     as the hills.
I was saved the same amount of times by your God as
     mine.
How useless death's been to me. Go ahead, time us.

Wellington, January 29, 2010

Any of the woefulness, low-blows
not signed into law, papering the walls
of my heart, were used to either pad
my libretto or slow down the aspirations
of our den's ancient drapes.
I tried not to swallow my tears,
but what hadn't been stolen
had been entered as such.
It seems much of what rates
as intolerable for me has been mostly
lost on you, tossed to those emptiest of lots.
Tomorrow, men with rat tails, purplish
tats, will start replacing the old tar.
We will sit in our cars, plates of grapes
on our laps, race forms slapped limp,
while the sun morphs into fool's gold
and we dig how the clouds glide
like the wonder our gods have outsourced.
Plovers move in accomplished loops
as they're lowered onto the polo grounds.

What's not to love of their ether-notes
and grins that we wring from them?
Those who aren't swept south in packs
are left to stew in their pens, just scrape by,
their sorrow multiplied by a thousand.
I have taken up teething again,
giddy upping on fence posts, half-naked
though the gnats have me tagged
as "tip-top" and the humidity's 3-D.
Nope, the past has never had
the least bit of patience with me.
But what's fated has no memory afterwards.
So I'll slip the first of many apples I'll fist
by the scent of clipped fuchsia, electric fence,
and tense up as the pony's lips crinkle,
its teeth clacking like something spring-loaded,
then feel the air it dismisses braid my wrist-hairs
as I look into its worried eyes and see
my deaths drowned, one in each pool.

Winter Rental

After backlogging last week's losses
I lob the whole book into the sea.
You could easily see me from any window
but the one in the kitchen with the niche
beneath the sill where you hid your secrets.
Retired, I shape putty into the littlest of whales
and laugh as the cat swipes at them, riveted
while you pull out your apron like a safety net,
knuckles scored from the table's edge,
before grabbing for the spyglass
keeping look out for that barge
with its belly of scrap paper, art.
I can taste brine, a billion lies going bad,
but this too is garbage, ad-libbed on the deck.
A military jet passes, a red X on its chest,
a gray similar to all the black and white
ever compromised, made to play nice,
its shrill cry a baby hawk's or a ghoul's.
You're wondering if it's still possible
to drown under miles of words,
stirring only to sit even further inside
the British floor-model version of yourself.
Is it there that you touch the one thing

that serves only your soul, the non-existent?
I feel slipshod and blowsy just mentioning it,
my teeth and tongue bent on my throat,
wanting none of this pinned on them.

Writer's Block

I see your winter's up for sale once again,
that you've come down in price on its eternal chill
and cold rain, this ice like a diabolical lace –
will even settle for less than you first paid,
and accept straw or diapers, a couple of candles,
even lease it out, and instead of a contract
have us scrawl our initials onto the kitchen's frosted glass
or score the sealskin that hangs near your desk
till some ink can be rescued from out the white –
thawed at that one path the fist still allows.

The Abduction

Afterwards – bedlam

cardinals descending
everywhere,
fate gyrating,

heaven's inked –
juxtaposing
knees, liturgies

mentioning nothing
of peculiar quiet,
reddened snows,

trumpeting!
Universal vocabulary's
whimpering, x'd,

yielding – zeros.

Broadcasting
to Robert Dunn

When that cold enters the room again,
stupefied, half-consumed with blue –
an intruder that has come to be all
too familiar with the layout of our brains,
we can only wonder who has sent it
and why its odor is that of a cave's,
its speech so much older than syllable, tense,
and why we'll soon arise and cloud the window
with inference but resist drawing that childish glyph,

coughing instead and resting our heads,
turning back once again to where our bodies
had curled, questioning, on the unmade bed,
our memories awash with the slumberous red of the sun;
memo: a light not convinced of itself and saying little
of the light that has been and the light yet to come
or the god on the sill freshly shaved in borrowed shoes
whose message we'll always miss as we think
about bliss then look down at what we've written about it,

though considering how the hour grows horns,
its laughter piped in through a century's wires,
it's probably best we're resigned to that spot on the glass
where we'll have reigned like a giant or an ant king,
and through which we're now zeroing in on this crow
we'd known first by its chuckling, crow-squawks,
and then by how we saw every crow that was
ever created superimposed onto this crow –
testing, check one, and then that crow, check two.

Birdwatching for Beginners

Though nothing's been notched off
the life list for weeks now –
except for those freaks from next door
with their fake grass and rakes,
their golf carts and odd humming,
their muddied and doomed owl-dummies
and my weeds all gummed up with dew –
I can still hear a cardinal acting up
in the leftover dark of the forest
exclaiming its life a small miracle
and this line-up of oft-ailing doves
ardently denying their lowliness.
To sit is to lobby one's own thoughts
as if deaf to the world and its air raids,
its laser-fed tumors and its fire sales,
the endless details of our own end
never laid to rest or fully believed in, but
to not sit's to opt out and stop it too soon,
put it up too happy-go-luckily in Tupperware.
Once, half-tipsy I'd stirred up enough
spit to work out a few trifling words,
to be answerable for at least my own breaths –
but of late, I've been looked-after, tailed,

the same crow the same dash between
shadows, the same assumption of ash yet again.
I'm afraid of their lot. But a bit more my own.
The look-a-likes who would kill for my bowl,
the teeth-torn dime roll at the tollbooth.
Or worse, the ones I keep spotting in the tree,
their nonstop love of overdone symbolism
nailed again and again to some limb.

Chatter

First, the tongue of the kingfisher
shifts in the throat and then it is given
to fits as if throttling consonants,
re-tasting its last descent, header.
Time after time, it stiffens the hairs
of death's ears with its mighty din –
teaching us no matter how offensive
or oft-tined the note, no matter its destiny,
might it not ignite into some kind of chord,
scoring the wind with the still-yet-untamed?

For Lack of Closure

That one second, the sea was the color of slate
and my to-go cup of tea had gone to smog.

But not even you or that crow that woke saddled
with night could talk me down from the tower.

I've got an acre of droppings and rocks
that need to be raked with incomprehensible care.

And my fingernails look slain with curry –
an older, more storied gold, than my ring.

How is it, the lost-then-found doubles in meaning
while the what-won't-ever-be still holds out for one?

I locate case studies in these sorts of details
but any antidotes are come upon much too late.

So, so much for the cat spilling out on your lap
licking itself far too skillfully for our liking.

And the petals, like wet condoms, stuck to the sill.
You will roll over, volunteering yet another sigh,

getting that look like you're thinking of leaving –
this cutest of grins suctioned into your veil.

Something ghostly threads through the door lock.
I take a cocktail sword to where my heart was.

A Bedtime Story
for Richard Barnes

We fell asleep with the laws of the jungle and were woken
up to the ones of the walled-in, declawed.

We fell asleep superstars and were woken up step-children,
pets – these cramped and tepid acts they kept imagining
they'd pat sparks from.

We fell asleep roaming our great grandparent's landmass –
their mountains and moors, and were woken up in a room
where we're part artifact and part fun fact, categorically
trapped with their janitor's carts and remotes their hand
sanitizers and charts.

We fell asleep in the lap of a hundred pasts and were woken
up where even the trees had to put up with this Tupperware
air, these unsettling suns.

We fell asleep with the most unsightly of holes and were
woken up sewn-tight, something woefully new, our stom-
achs eternally sated, long-forgetting the taste of the leaf,
how it feels on the tongue.

We fell asleep roofless, nearly gaining on angels, and were woken up slain again, ironed-out into angles, then nailed to the floor.

We fell asleep eaten and bit-into and were woken up dined-on and nibbled, billed high in undesirable fat.

We fell asleep known-to-ourselves and well-practiced in blood and were woken as our doubles – these memories clouding up, pelts.

We fell asleep likened to poetry – leap-taking and skilled, and were woken up clichés they peeled back from this plastic, stuck-pinned and then saw to again and again until flawless.

We fell asleep testy and thrashing and were woken up yet-at-peace and expertly voiced-over.

We fell asleep a-sea or unspooling into night and were woken, tape-loops tuned into soft rock, the automaton's set list.

We fell asleep these shit-covered heaps and were woken up lab-coats texting ourselves.

We fell asleep in the shadows of a few doped-up,
un-worshipped gods and were woken drop-lit, prodded
into the poses of show dogs.

We fell asleep not conversant in in-ground pools, gates,
and digestive aids and were woken up in stages, then
staple-gunned and tagged.

We fell asleep mumbling, bum-legged and dented-up,
and were woken up merely legends.

Acknowledgements

I am grateful to the editors of these journals where these poems first appeared:

2 Bridges Review, American Journal of Poetry, apt, basalt, BlazeVOX, The Café Review, Coconut, Fogged Clarity, Gargoyle, Ghost Town, Grey, Hamilton Stone Review, Hunger Mountain, Jet Fuel Magazine, La Fovea, Map Literary, The Milo Review, Mojo, Nixes Mate Review, Off the Coast, one, SAND: Berlin's English Literary Journal, St. Petersburg Review, San Pedro River Review, Sliver of Stone Magazine, Stillwater Review, Stone Coast Review, Thin Air, thrush.

About the Author

Born in Lowell Massachusetts in 1960, Mark DeCarteret graduated from Emerson College with a B.F.A. in Creative Writing in 1990, where he was selected by Bill Knott as their representative at the Greater Boston Inter-collegiate Poetry Festival, and from the University of New Hampshire with an M.A. in English-Writing in 1993, where he was selected by Mekeel McBride and Charles Simic for the Thomas Williams Memorial Poetry Prize. He's published five books of poetry and has appeared in nearly 400 literary reviews including *AGNI, Boston Review, Caliban, Chicago Review, Conduit, Confrontation, Cream City Review, Diagram, Poetry East, Salamander,* as well as anthologies such as *American Poetry: The Next Generation* (Carnegie Mellon Press), *Thus Spake the Corpse: An Exquisite Corpse Reader 1988-1998* (Black Sparrow Press), and *Under the Legislature of Stars: 62 New Hampshire Poets* (Oyster River Press), which he also co-edited. Mark served as Portsmouth, New Hampshire's seventh Poet Laureate from 2009-2011 and currently works at Water Street Bookstore in Exeter.

42° 19′ 47.9″ N   70° 56′ 43.9″ W

Nixes Mate is a navigational hazard in Boston Harbor used during the colonial period to gibbet and hang pirates and mutineers.

Nixes Mate Books features small-batch artisanal literature, created by writers who use all 26 letters of the alphabet and then some, honing their craft the time-honored way: one line at a time.

nixesmate.pub/books